The Little
Book of
Resilience

This book is dedicated to my friends,
Joanna Francis and Joanna Codrai,
two of the most resilient
(and brilliant) people I know.

The Little
Book of
Resilience

Cheryl Rickman

An Hachette UK Company
www.hachette.co.uk

First published in Great Britain in 2019 by Gaia Books,
an imprint of Octopus Publishing Group Ltd
Carmelite House
50 Victoria Embankment
London EC4Y 0DZ
www.octopusbooks.co.uk

Distributed in the US by Hachette Book Group,
1290 Avenue of the Americas, 4th and 5th Floors, New York, NY 10104

Distributed in Canada by Canadian Manda Group
664 Annette Street, Toronto, Ontario, Canada M6S 2C8

ISBN 978-1-85675-397-5

A CIP catalogue record for this book is available from the British Library.

Printed and bound in China.

10 9 8 7 6 5 4 3 2 1

Publishing Director Stephanie Jackson
Art Director Juliette Norsworthy
Senior Editor Alex Stetter
Copy Editor Katy Denny
Design and illustrations Abi Read
Senior Production Controller Allison Gonsalves

Contents

Introduction

Life isn't a bed of roses. Our days are rarely hassle free, and we all encounter difficulties – both big and small. Many adversities are as universal as they are inevitable. Some seem insurmountable: devastating loss, tragic illness, life-changing injury. Other obstacles seem more possible to overcome: rejection, divorce, failure.

Some are expected, others take us completely by surprise. Either way, hardships cause us to feel heartbroken and shocked, disappointed and depressed. And sometimes, it isn't a terrible event or huge hardship with which we struggle, but the daily hassles of everyday life, which can generate a cumulative toll on our brains.

When faced with a challenge, whatever its size, what do we do next? How do we respond to a crushing blow? How do we cope and persevere? Is it possible to bounce back to where we were before? Can we ever be happy again? If so, how? When it looks as if life will never be the same again, what do we do to recover? And, when we find ourselves overwhelmed with daily challenges, how do we best react?

The good news, even when we're in the midst of bad news, is we can learn to hope and cope when all seems lost. For it is how we *respond* to what happens to us that impacts the trajectory of our lives. This means we can get through whatever life throws at us, however devastating or relentless.

Humans have the inbuilt capacity to survive adversity and go on to thrive. This little book explores the steps we can take, tools we can equip ourselves with and techniques we can master to overcome life's unexpected challenges, no matter how big or impossible they may seem. This book also explores the concept of post-traumatic growth and how it is possible to find deeper meaning and greater strength *because* of an adversity experience, not despite it.

Of course, while hardships are common, not everyone has experienced tragedy. Resilience can be built regardless of what has or hasn't happened to you. You can build resilience long before life-changing adversity hits. We need resilience to cope with the smaller daily challenges we all face too.

Indeed, everybody needs resilience, not just to deal with the tough stuff, but to boost our levels of life satisfaction and improve our performance. So says over 50 years of scientific research. How much resilience we have is a key determinant of how happy and successful we are likely to be.

Whatever you have been through or will go through in life, no matter how big or small, you are not alone. And that's important. Us humans, we're in this together.

This book sets out to use our universal human experiences of adversity to help each other better **RESPOND, RECOVER** and **RISE**.

1. What is Resilience?

'My barn having burned down,
I can now see the moon.'

MIZUTA MASAHIDE,
SEVENTEENTH-CENTURY JAPANESE POET AND SAMURAI

Finding Resilience

Life is a journey. The bumps in the road are many, and the inevitable twists and turns, ups and downs along the way have the potential to derail us.

Resilience is our engine.

It helps keep us going and driving forward through the thickest mud and along the grittiest paths, rather than veering off track, getting stuck or lost.

Respond Well

How we handle hardships and hassles en route determines how resilient we are. And how we respond to the obstacles on our path determines whether or not we are able to enjoy the journey.

This is resilience – our capacity to cope, our response to adversity, our ability to recover and rise.

'In the middle of difficulty
lies opportunity.'

ALBERT EINSTEIN

Struggles Strengthen Us

Interestingly, the more bumps in the road we face on our journey, the better we get at steering along tricky passages and driving on through the wildest of storms. The more difficult the route, the more practiced we become. In this way, overcoming challenges has actually been found to be necessary to truly flourish.

We have the capacity to become mentally stronger than we were before adversity strikes. That's how our physical health works too: if we break a bone, our body works to make that bone stronger than it was before it broke.

We are wired to be resilient physically and mentally, even when faced with significant life traumas. We have within us the capacity to cope with even the most brutal blows, when tragic events change the trajectory of our lives (and us) forever.

Yet, we are less naturally equipped to deal with the smaller yet frequent stressors in our everyday lives. These require a different type of mental toughness; a certain adaptability and flexibility; something that most of us aren't trained in.

> 'Difficulties are things that show a person what they are.'
>
> EPICTETUS

Mind Gym

Before the 1970s resilience was seen as a character trait, a kind of internal strength which you either had or you didn't. Thankfully, we now know resilience is a teachable mental skill set that everyone can develop. Just as we can strengthen our physical muscles by going to the gym, we can strengthen our resilience with training and personal mastery.

We know resilience is teachable because scientists have studied children who've overcome great odds to thrive in adulthood. As well as having someone to support them, children who thrived in the face of adversity had a different mindset and way of handling challenges than those who didn't thrive. This process of 'behavioural adaptation' is resilience. And it comes both from within us and from support outside of us.

It wasn't the circumstances the children faced that determined how resilient they were, it was how they *thought* and *felt* about those circumstances and what they did next. Their **thoughts, feelings and actions** held the key to their resilience, and thus their freedom to enjoy life.

Intentional Response

These findings have enabled positive psychology researchers to establish how a resilient mindset can be taught; to define how, when we get knocked down, we can get back up again.

Researchers have found that life circumstances and genetics only partially determine our levels of happiness: 40 per cent of our life satisfaction comes down to the intentional activities we participate in; that is to say what we **think**, how we **feel** and what we **do**.

They found that when adversity strikes, we can avoid the void of despair or, at the very least, ease the anguish. Through our thoughts, feelings and actions, we can flex our resilience muscles and clamber back out from the darkest depths of despair to find light, hope and even joy.

Stronger Than you Think

As Sheryl Sandberg says in her book with Adam Grant, *Option B*, '[Resilience] isn't about having a backbone. It's about strengthening the muscles around our backbone.' And Sandberg should know. In May 2015 her husband died suddenly, but she and her family were able to navigate through the acute grief and come out the other side.

We often only realize how strong we are when being strong is our only option. This is the journey of resilience. It takes us from anguish and pain toward hope and happiness. Moments that make the heart sink can be replaced with moments that make the heart sing. And, as we wade through the murky parts of the journey, we build those muscles around our backbone and grow stronger. We can all learn to cope better, hope better and 'struggle well' (see page 30).

Taking the Wheel

Resilience isn't about
ignoring sadness or pushing
stress away, it's about learning
to navigate our negative
emotions and find a way
through them.

Often, we're unable to change the
challenges we face, but we can change ourselves and how we
respond to those challenges. Resilience enables us to get
back in the driver's seat of our lives after we've been thrown
off course. It enables us to regain control and lessen the
impact of adversity as we move forward, so we may
overcome difficulties more readily, cope more effectively and
cherish all that we still have to be grateful for more brightly.

Resilience gives us the opportunity to lean in to our sadness
and embrace our fear, so we may choose hope, meaning and
joy; so we may recover, rise and grow.

Why Resilience Matters

There are some things we all aspire to be –
happy, successful, healthy, resilient.
We don't, as a rule, aspire to be
less any of these things. The
added bonus with resilience
is that it has the power to
have a positive impact on
these other aspirations
as well.

'If you're going
through hell,
keep going.'

WINSTON CHURCHILL

Resilience Makes Us Happier

Resilience makes us less depressed and anxious. It also makes us happier.

🌿 The Penn Resilience Programme, a study into preventing depression and anxiety in children, revealed that participants were less anxious and had fewer depressive symptoms than those in the control group. Behavioural problems reduced while physical health, wellbeing and optimism increased, even years later.

🌿 The Healthy Minds Curriculum trialled in 34 schools across England in 2014–18 significantly improved life satisfaction among participating teachers and children.

🌿 In their 2013 paper 'Psychological Resilience', researchers Mustafa Sarkar and David Fletcher reported research findings that those with high resilience scores had higher self-efficacy, autonomy, flexibility and creativity, so felt more in control and capable than those with low resilience scores. They also exhibited greater optimism and better problem-solving and stress-management skills. Resilience is an 'ordinary magic' that leads to extraordinary performance.

Positivity Fuels Resilience: Broaden and Build Theory

The findings of positive psychology researcher Barbara Fredrickson suggest that positive emotions (such as gratitude, love and awe) in the aftermath of a crisis buffer resilient people against depression and enable them to thrive.

Fredrickson came up with the 'broaden and build' theory: when we experience positive emotions, our cognitive abilities are improved and BROADEN, making us more open to possibilities and solutions. (Conversely, negative emotions close down our capacity to think straight and cloud our judgement.)

Resilience is one part of what psychologists call 'psychological capital'. Other parts include optimism, hope and self-efficacy - the belief that we can handle a challenge based on our own strengths. When we have a good stock of psychological capital to tap into, we are better able to learn new information and develop both physical and mental strength. Our ability to make new bonds and solidify existing ones is also improved, along with our sense of identity and purpose. We can use the reserves of positive emotions that we BUILD up as a form of currency, to save during easier times or spend during tougher times.

Rather than glossing over negative thoughts or experiences or ignoring threats, topping up our reserve banks with positive emotions helps us see adversities, process them and figure out ways to move past them.

Studies show that as well as helping us to cope better with life, resilience enables us to:

- Stay calm under pressure.

- Reduce and better handle anxiety.

- Experience less depression.

- Identify and solve problems with greater ease.

- Accurately read social cues.

- Believe in our ability to succeed.

- Make better decisions.

Resilience Helps Us Make Better Decisions

Being able to think clearly helps us choose wisely when we encounter difficulties in our lives. In turbulent times, it's easy to default to what distracts and numbs us – endless episodes of our favourite TV programmes, alcohol, drugs – anything that provides an escape route from our problems. However, as we know (but sometimes choose to ignore), running away from our troubles relinquishes our power over them. Numbing ourselves makes us unable to move forward. Conversely, resilience puts us back in the driving seat.

This sense of control gives us the ability to cope with grief, stress and anxiety and provides us with an inner strength to take risks, bolster optimism and reject inaccurate and negative self-talk or criticism.

In contrast to numbing, resilience is about leaning in to what we are feeling, experiencing pain and failure and loss. It's about falling down but keeping going. It's about choosing self-compassion and self-acceptance in order to assume control and move through those feelings to emerge on the other side.

Resilience Improves Our Emotional Regulation and Functionality

Sadness and anger are perfectly healthy emotions. They give us the opportunity to release stress hormones like cortisol by expressing tears and rage. However, sometimes we can get stuck in an emotion. When we get stuck in worry it becomes anxiety, which prevents us from solving the problems we're worried about. Getting stuck in sadness prevents us from fully participating in life.

When the emotional, irrational part of our brain is engaged, our logical brain takes a back seat. When we feel them, express them and move through them, all emotions are a natural and helpful part of what it means to be human. But when we get stuck in emotions, our cognitive abilities are reduced and we are less able to function.

By learning resilience skills, such as how to talk back to our thoughts in real time to gain perspective (see page 50) and how to use our breathing to stay calm (see page 66), we can move through our emotions, so we can stay on track.

Resilience Makes Us Grittier

Another way resilience increases our chances of success is by fuelling our grit.

Resilience matters because it helps us continue to rise; not only to overcome obstacles but to reach our potential and generate the wellbeing that accomplishment, a key pillar of wellbeing, gives us.

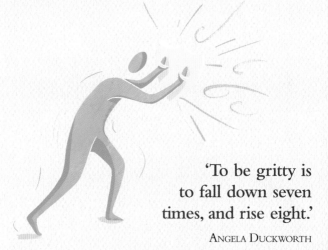

'To be gritty is to fall down seven times, and rise eight.'

ANGELA DUCKWORTH

Here are five ways to grow your grit:

- **Challenge yourself.** Set yourself a daily challenge of exceeding your previous abilities in order to build up your skill level.

- **Choose to persevere rather than quit.** Each time you do you'll earn the double reward of achieving a goal and proving that you have what it takes to do so.

- **Try new things.** This bolsters your tolerance for uncertainty and demonstrates that with uncertainty comes possibility.

- **Push yourself to do tricky tasks in tiny bouts.** Move them to the top of your to-do list and get them done in small doses. Break daunting tasks into bite-size chunks, and tackle a little bit every day.

- **Get creative with alternative ways to achieve your goals**. For example, if you want to get fit and spend more time with friends, synchronize these tasks by going on a bike ride *with* your friends. Want to learn a new language and get fitter but can't afford classes? Download an audio book and listen to it while you walk.

Resilience Makes Us Stronger

Adversity provides us with opportunities to flex our resilience muscles. The more practice a race car driver has, the better he or she becomes at handling the track. Similarly, the more we practise rising to challenges, the better we become at handling life.

Research in 2010 about cumulative adversity in relation to resilience shows we benefit from being challenged. Just as our muscles grow stronger when we use them, so our mind grows stronger when we use our resilience.

Knowing that with each challenge we have the capacity to grow stronger is empowering. It can enable us to see all of life as wonderful, even the toughest times, and more readily enjoy our unique journeys.

Stress, grief, anxiety and depression can be debilitating. But resilience skills can help those suffering to emerge from these states like a butterfly emerging from its cocoon. The possibility for growth exists within us all. See more on post-traumatic growth on page 71.

2. How to Respond

'The brain is like Velcro for negative experiences but Teflon for positive ones.'

RICK HANSON, NEUROSCIENTIST

Why Our Thoughts Matter

Renowned psychologist Chris Peterson described
resilience as our ability to 'struggle well'. But what does
struggling well feel like? Resilient people tend to feel
hopeful about situations, rather than hopeless. They tend
to accept what they can't change and change what they can.
And they tend to feel
capable as opposed
to incapable.

A lot of this comes
down to perception
and response.
So, in building
resilience, to
feel differently,
we need to
think differently.

Our Negativity Bias

As humans, we are wired for positivity but conditioned for negativity. We have an inbuilt negativity bias which, according to neuroscientists, means we have a tendency to focus on – and react more strongly to – negative comments, situations or events.

Critical, cautious and judgemental thoughts used to serve us well back when sabre-toothed tigers lurked around the corner. If we noticed the leaves rustling, it was far better to assume the worst and avoid danger than assume the best and meet a gruesome end. Nowadays, such caution and pessimism are less helpful.

But isn't what we *do* more important than what we *think*? After all, our thoughts are only thoughts, not facts, so surely it doesn't matter what we think…does it?

Do Thoughts Create Beliefs That Create Behaviour?

What we *do* is important, but our thoughts, beliefs, feelings and actions are intrinsically linked. In fact, our thoughts create our beliefs which, in turn, generate how we perceive and respond to circumstances. Each time we repeat a thought, neurons fire together to create neural pathways of beliefs, and those beliefs cause us to behave or respond in a certain way – thoughts become beliefs that guide our behaviour. As such, what we *think* has a major influence on our re(actions); our beliefs determine what we actually do.

Our beliefs feed our actions. For instance, if you think you're a terrible cook, you're unlikely to bother practising. Then, if you *do* try, you're unlikely to be happy with the results because you've not made the effort to improve. So, your belief that you're a terrible cook becomes a self-fulfilling prophecy, proving you right and cementing your belief.

Whereas, if you believe cooking is a skill that can be developed, and think, 'I'm not great at cooking *yet*,' you would devote time to honing your skills. Over time, you'd cook better food.

This is why people who have a 'growth mindset', rather than a 'fixed mindset', tend to be more resilient. They attribute a failure as specific to a certain event ('I failed at cooking *that* dish') rather than attributable to character failings ('I'm a failure at cooking. I *always* mess up'). They see failures as opportunities to grow and learn and believe they can improve with practice.

Thankfully, our neural networks are not set in stone. Thanks to our neuroplasticity we can change our thoughts and our thinking style and, in doing so, shift our beliefs (and our subsequent actions and reactions) – see pages 52–63.

When Life Gives You Lemons, Make Lemonade

When we see mistakes as chances to learn, stressful times as opportunities to test our resolve and obstacles as ways to find out more about ourselves, we can turn tough times into insightful knowledge and we can find the good in the worst.

By choosing how we respond, we can attribute value to *all* our experiences; both those we enjoy and those we endure.

For example, mistakes equip us with knowledge we may not have had if we hadn't made the mistake in the first place. When we see mistakes as opportunities to learn, we are less likely to beat ourselves up about making them.

🌿 Consider all you've learned from adversity. List ways you have learned from the past to build knowledge to help you in the future.

🌿 Imagine you're late for an appointment and find yourself stuck in a traffic jam. You can't change the situation, but you can change how you respond. Whether you get stressed and beep your horn, or instead breathe deeply, message your client and listen to an audio book while you wait, the traffic will remain. The first reaction will rile you up and ruin your mood. The second will calm you down and give you back control. It will also enable you to make the most of quiet time you wouldn't have had were it not for the line of cars stretching out in front of you.

Our Perception Drives
Our Reaction

How well we respond to, recover from and rise
following adversity often comes down to our perception
of the challenge itself.
According to resilience
expert Karen Reivich, we
can boost our resilience
by changing the way we
think about adversity.

'There is nothing
either good or bad,
but thinking makes it so.'

WILLIAM SHAKESPEARE, *HAMLET*

Explanatory Style and Causal Analysis: Why Things Happen

When it comes to resilience, how we explain to ourselves WHAT is happening (interpretation), WHY it's happening (attribution) and what might happen NEXT (expectation) tells us a lot about our belief system.

How we habitually explain *why* good and bad events in our lives happen to us – the reason or cause of a setback or success – is known as our 'explanatory style'. Fortunately, this is learned (we either experience learned hopelessness or learned optimism), which means it can be changed.

The goal of changing our explanatory style is to cultivate more flexible and accurate thinking and to move from learned hopelessness toward learned optimism, a key component of resilience. After all, being stuck in a style of thinking which is inaccurate doesn't serve us well.

The Three Ps: Stunting or Enabling Recovery

Essentially, optimistic and pessimistic thinkers will explain why something has happened to them differently. Consequently, optimistic thinkers will briskly bounce back from troubles and stay motivated when they succeed, whereas pessimistic thinkers may buckle under pressure and see successes as a fluke.

After 30 years of study, Martin Seligman discovered the 'three Ps' of explanatory style – **P**ersonalization, **P**ervasiveness and **P**ermanence – can stunt our recovery from setbacks via our belief that either we're at fault (Personalization); that something will last forever (Permanence) and/or will affect all areas of our lives (Pervasiveness) – see opposite for examples.

If you currently fit into the more pessimistic thinking style, remember it's possible to change this by reframing and cultivating a more optimistic mindset. Once we see that hardships aren't our fault, won't spill over into every area of life and won't last forever, we are better able to cope with those challenges. We can struggle better.

PESSIMISTIC THINKERS	OPTIMISTIC THINKERS
TEND TO SEE SETBACKS AS:	**TEND TO SEE SETBACKS AS:**
Down to them and their faults **(personalized: caused by internal factors)**	*Not entirely their fault* **(caused by external factors)**
Long-lasting **(permanent)**	*Unlikely to last* **(temporary)**
Likely to undermine everything they do **(pervasive and global)**	*Specific and isolated to a particular circumstance* **(local)**
YET THEY SEE THEIR SUCCESSES AS:	**YET THEY SEE THEIR SUCCESSES AS:**
Total coincidences and lucky flukes **(caused by external factors)**	*Down to them and their hard work/effort* **(personalized: caused by internal factors)**
Unlikely to last **(temporary)**	*Long-lasting and sustainable* **(permanent)**
Specific and isolated to a particular circumstance **(local)**	*Likely to spill over to other areas of their lives* **(pervasive and global)**

Know What You Can Control

Understanding what is within your control and what isn't helps build a resilient mindset. For example, you can control your goals, your effort, your behaviour, who you spend time with, how you take care of yourself and what you think and do. You can't control what others say, think or do, past mistakes, or circumstances and situations that happen to you.

The Seven Factors of Resilience

According to Karen Reivich and Andrew Shatté, authors of *The Resilience Factor*, we each have a resilience quotient, which is measurable. We can identify our own thinking style by understanding what they call the Seven Factors of Resilience, each of which is buildable.

The Seven Factors of Resilience are:

1. **Emotion Regulation** (our ability to stay calm under pressure).

2. **Impulse Control** (our ability to control our behaviour, tolerate ambiguity, plan responses and delay gratification so we may stay focused, persistent and aware).

3. **Causal Analysis or Explanatory Style** (our ability to gain perspective over any given situation and think accurately and flexibly regarding the causes and implications of events, so we may see setbacks as temporary and caused by external factors).

4. **Self-efficacy** (how in control we feel when problem-solving and rising to challenges).

5. **Realistic Optimism** (how much we realistically believe things can change for the better and that problems are often caused by circumstances beyond our control, yet can be solved by us, plus our ability to find the good in negative situations).

6. **Empathy** (our ability to read social cues and empathize with other people's emotional states so we can gain a better sense of unity and 'being in this together').

7. **Reaching Out** (how comfortable we feel reaching out to others and accepting social support, and how likely we are to try new things and rise to challenges).

Each of these Seven factors is governed by how we think.

And it is how we think which governs how quickly we recover. So, about that...

3. How To Recover

'The bamboo that bends is stronger than the oak that resists.'

JAPANESE PROVERB

Getting Your Facts Straight

A thought is, essentially, neurons firing. The more we repeat an individual thought, the stronger the neural connections become, creating neural networks of beliefs. This means, the more we repeat a thought, the stronger our beliefs become.

Inaccurate Thinking

The problem is that our thoughts aren't always accurate. In fact, our thoughts and subsequent beliefs are often the result of conditioning. The world (parents, teachers, peers, media) has a habit of telling us who we should be/become and what to believe. Consequently, other people's opinions influence our own and determine how we think, so, as children, we draw inaccurate conclusions. These are repeated, so become beliefs about who we are and influence our judgements, concerns and ongoing mind-chatter.

Our more pessimistic thoughts tend to be inaccurate and inflexible, in part due to negativity bias, which skews our perception. Indeed, our lives and ourselves tend to be much better than we believe them to be!

Despite this, we rarely consider questioning our thoughts, even when those thoughts may be cruel, pessimistic or inaccurate. Yet, just because someone believes they're inadequate or unlucky or unemployable, it doesn't mean it's true, because thoughts are not facts.

Inflexible Thinking

When we become stuck in a single story, we lose our flexibility, and when we lose our flexibility, we lose our resilience. To bolster our resilience, we can use strategies to ensure our thoughts are factual, helpful and flexible.

Resilience training teaches us to distance ourselves from our pessimistic explanations so that we may verify their accuracy.

To do so, we need to learn to argue with ourselves.

The Cognitive ABC Model

A is the Adverse event

B is the Belief

C is the Consequence
of having that belief
(that is to say, how
we respond via
our actions)

The relationship between
thoughts, feelings and
actions forms the basic
premise of cognitive
behavioural therapy (CBT).
We can use a model from
CBT, which takes the lens
through which we see the
world and fine-tunes it,
to positively impact our
responses and behaviour.

To build our resilience, CBT takes how we respond to
adversity (A) then questions and reframes our belief (B)
around that adverse event to shift how we feel and
subsequently behave (C). Psychologists call this the Cognitive
ABC Model.

Do You Know Your ABCs?

Let's say you don't get chosen for the football team.
That's the adverse event (A). Your belief (B) i.e. how
you interpret that adversity and attribute the cause of it,

PESSIMISTIC THINKERS	OPTIMISTIC THINKERS
ADVERSITY:	**ADVERSITY:**
Not chosen for the team.	*Not chosen for the team.*
BELIEF:	**BELIEF:**
I'm not skilled enough. *I'll never be any good.* *Feel disappointed.*	*I didn't practise enough.* *If I practise more I'll have a* *better chance. Feel determined.*
CONSEQUENCE:	**CONSEQUENCE:**
Give up playing football.	*Practise more so you might* *be selected next time.*

will affect your feelings and behaviours from that point onward, i.e. the consequence of your belief (C).

When you get to know your habitual thought process in response to adversities, you are effectively tuning in to your internal mind-chatter, your personal radio station. You can then separate the facts around the adversity (A) from the thoughts and beliefs being played out in your internal radio station (B) and understand how it makes you behave (C).

Once you are able to do this you'll be able to reconsider your thoughts to create a better response and outcome.

ACTIVITY:
Consider the Facts

A. Think about a setback you've experienced. Write down the facts of what happened (for example, I wasn't picked for the team/choir/course/job). ....
....
....

B. What thoughts and beliefs popped into your head about why that happened? ....
....
....

C. What were the consequences? How did you feel and what did you do in reaction to the setback? ....
....
....

Can you generate any alternative beliefs which may be more accurate? Are there any actions which may have served you better? When you consider the facts, can you dispute the beliefs you had about that adversity with evidence to the contrary?

Disputing the Evidence to Increase Optimism and Hope

By fact-checking and seeking evidence to dispute and reframe our beliefs, we can literally change our minds and grow our resilience.

Look at it this way: if somebody else falsely accuses you of being terrible at something, you will likely list all the reasons they are wrong. Yet, when you self-criticize and judge yourself in the same way, you're less likely to dispute those pessimistic thoughts, even when they are false.

The cognitive intervention of talking back to your thoughts is called 'reframing' and enables you to respond to inaccurate thoughts and inflexible beliefs that don't serve you, by countering and challenging them.

On the following pages, we will look at how to shift your less resilient thinking and belief patterns to build your resilience.

Cognitive Reframing: The Process

There are two types of thought that prevent resilience.

1. **Judgemental thoughts** (about why an adverse event has happened). In other words, our interpretations and attribution.

2. **Worries** (about what might happen next). In other words, our expectations.

Both types of detrimental thoughts can be reframed by using the following cognitive reframing process.

1. **BECOME CALM AND FOCUSED** so you can think rationally.

2. **TUNE IN TO YOUR INTERNAL RADIO STATION** so you can get to know your mind-chatter and identify beliefs.

3. **TAKE YOUR THOUGHTS TO COURT**. Dispute false thoughts and beliefs (judgements) with evidence to the contrary.

4. **GET PERSPECTIVE**. Calm anxious thoughts (worries) by fact-checking and considering the most likely outcome.

5. **CREATE MORE ACCURATE BELIEF STATEMENTS** by talking back to negative, inaccurate thoughts and false beliefs using cognitive reframing and real-time resilience.

6. **EVALUATE ACCURACY OF REFRAMED THOUGHTS** by passing them through the 'gut test' (see page 63), then **OBSERVE THE ENERGY SHIFT** which comes from disputing and replacing your negative beliefs.

Let's work through each of these steps one by one.

1. Become Calm and Focused

To think clearly, it's important to be calm. When we feel stressed, our brain goes into fight-or-flight mode. This means we're less able to think rationally when we most need to.

The best ways to access our rational brain are to calm ourselves down and focus our attention away from the negative beliefs. Here's how:

- Take three deep breaths – breathe in for a count of four, hold and then breathe out for a count of five.

- Count backward from 100 by 7. So 100, 93, 86 and so on... Doing so helps you to flick the switch from emotional brain to rational brain.

- Focus your attention on your senses – think about what you can hear, see, smell, touch and/or taste.

- Name every school teacher you've ever had, or memorize and recite a poem with an uplifting message.

These calming and focusing strategies help you think more rationally, so you are better positioned to talk back to your mind-chatter and beat intrusive negative thoughts.

2. Tune in to Your Internal Radio Station

The more aware we are about our habitual thought patterns and the type of language our internal mind-chatter uses, the better we become at working with our more inaccurate and inflexible thoughts by countering them with antidotes.

In their two-decade study of resilience, Karen Reivich and Andrew Shatté summarize the kind of thinking traps we all habitually fall into, from jumping to conclusions (assuming we know what a situation means, despite not having any evidence to support those assumptions) and tunnel vision (focusing on what we've done wrong and ignoring all we've done right) to mind reading (assuming we know what other people are thinking and/or expect other people to know what we're thinking, despite not having expressed themselves/ourselves).

The antidotes to these thinking traps are simply to slow down (breathe), ask questions, seek more evidence, consider the bigger picture and express ourselves clearly.

3. Take Your Thoughts to Court

When you dispute your thoughts by seeking evidence for and against them, you can cultivate more flexible thinking and more accurate belief systems.

Once you've identified your beliefs about a situation (for example, 'she doesn't care about me...nobody seems to lately' or 'I'm never going to find a job...I'm not skilled enough') you can take those thoughts to court. If there's even a shred of evidence against a thought, the thought is inaccurate so needs reframing.

Give thoughts around that belief an accuracy percentage (including the initial inaccurate one), then notice the energy you feel as you successfully counter your negative beliefs.

To practise using this handy disputation tool, repeat this exercise with the next three setbacks which occur in your daily life.

ACTIVITY:
Dispute Your Thoughts

YOUR TURN:

Jot down a belief or thought that's not serving you.

....

....

....

....

....

....

....

ACCURACY
PERCENTAGE

%

Seek evidence to dispute the belief, to prove that it's inaccurate.

....

....

....

....

....

....

....

ACCURACY
PERCENTAGE

%

4. Get Perspective

It's human nature to have 'what if' or 'what next' thoughts relating to the future; they're part of our survival instinct. Yet our worries can lead us to imagine unlikely worst-case scenarios and fall into spirals of catastrophic thinking.

Our worries start small but can grow, like a snowball that increases in size as it rolls downhill, with each thought building on the last. This 'snowball thinking' can cause irrational thoughts to feel accurate.

For example:

What if I fail this test?...I'll never get in to university...My parents will disown me...I'll never achieve anything...I'll fail at life!

All of this when you haven't even taken the test yet. And even if you did fail it, you could retake it, or end up working in a role completely unrelated to that test.

Your brain doesn't go straight from 'What if I fail this test?' to 'I'll fail at life'. It builds from one thought to the next, which tricks us into believing our catastrophic worries are rational thoughts. In reality, they are speculations based on false assumptions with no real content whatsoever.

With judgements we can take our thoughts to court and dispute our beliefs. But we can't see evidence for worries, because the future hasn't happened yet. We need a different approach. Once we're calm enough, we can:

- Schedule in some 'worry time'. If we park our worries to be dealt with and heard later, we can contain them and deal with them more calmly.

- Remind ourselves that we'll handle it, just like we've done in the past.

We can also gain perspective by:

- Fact-checking. When we focus our attention on the facts of the matter, rather than the possibilities of what might happen, we can gain perspective.

- Consider the worst-case, best-case and most likely scenarios and attribute a percentage of likelihood to them.

For example, imagine you are trying to move house and you start to worry when your buyer goes quiet. You imagine the worst possible scenario (your sale falls through, you lose your intended purchase and never find another house you like).

1. Give yourself permission to consider that unlikely worst-case scenario.

2. Now imagine an equally unlikely best-case scenario (Previous owners give you some amazing furniture).

3. Next, focus on the most likely scenario by considering the facts (your buyer is quiet, but hasn't gone away).

You can attribute a percentage of likelihood to each scenario:

🌿 Lose house and never find another one. (10 per cent)

🌿 Get house with bonus great furniture. (5 per cent)

🌿 Sale goes through within reasonable timescale. (85 per cent)

Worry won't make a problem better, but how you frame your thinking and respond to worrying thoughts will help you gain perspective and stay in a stronger, more resilient frame of mind. This cognitive tool helps us focus on the most realistic outcome. It's a great way to get everything into perspective and bring accuracy and flexibility into play.

Finally, consider whether there's anything you can do to help bring the most likely outcome to fruition.

5. Create More Accurate Belief Statements

If I asked you to stop thinking about a blue beach ball, all you'd be able to think about is a blue beach ball. That's down to our attention bias, which makes us see whatever we are thinking about, so our brains are unable to 'not think about something'. Similarly, if you tried pushing your thoughts away (like pushing the beach ball under the water), they'll just resurface later (just as the beach ball will pop back up). The only way to change our thoughts is to replace them with new reframed ones (akin to popping the blue beach ball and replacing it with a multi-coloured one).

Reframing and Real-time Resilience

The process of talking back to our mind-chatter as it happens is also known as 'real-time resilience'. Reframing our thoughts in the heat of the moment can take practice, so it's useful to work on reframing thoughts and beliefs using the cognitive reframing process and then, whenever you catch your mind chattering negatively, start using the tag lines listed below to talk back to those thoughts with the evidence you've collected.

For judgements:

🌿 'That's not true, because...'

🌿 'Another way of seeing that is...'

For worries:

🌿 'The most likely outcome is...'

🌿 'I can...'

For example: 'I'm never going to get a job I like' could be talked back to with, 'That's not true because I'm applying regularly for jobs that match my skill set. I found previous jobs within a month and I've only been looking for a week.'

6. Evaluate Accuracy of Reframed Thoughts and Observe the Energy Shift

Once you've replaced an inaccurate thought with a more accurate one, you can evaluate whether it passes the 'gut test' to ensure you're not replacing a wildly inaccurate negative statement with a wildly inaccurate positive statement.

For example, if your judgement was 'I'm terrible at painting' and you replaced that belief with 'I'm the best artist in town', they would both be inaccurate. A more valid reframe would be, 'Painting isn't one of my strengths, but I'm improving with practice.'

Finally, spend a moment noticing the energy that comes from successfully dealing with your negative beliefs. This will provide you with motivation to repeat the exercise again and again.

Give yourself a break

Other ways to recover more quickly from adversity are
to ramp up your self-care and practise mindfulness – both
will help your cognitive reframing come from a place
of calm consideration.

Recharge and Recover: Ramp Up Your Self-care

Stopping is an important strategy. Our brains need to rest
and recharge as much as our bodies do, so we need to give
them recovery periods.

Biology tells us that homeostasis (where the brain
continuously restores and sustains wellbeing) is only possible
when we stop and recover, in between periods of trying our
hardest to perform well. As such, one process of resilience in
basic form is: Try hard. Stop and recover. Persist.

If we want to perform well, recovery periods are essential.
Stopping work doesn't automatically equal recovery time as
we continue to look at screens and think about work. We
need to disengage fully in order to truly recover.

Create technology-free zones where you cannot access your phone (the average person looks at their phone 150 times per day – that's continuous cognitive arousal, with no real recovery time for the mind!).

Take regular relaxation breaks. Even stopping for one minute to look up and breathe slowly can impact positively how you feel and how you solve problems when they arise. Move away from your desk, sip water, breathe and relax.

Take calm action. Participate in activities which calm your mind and/or strengthen your body, such as yoga, Pilates, meditation and tai chi.

Go outside and let nature nourish you. Studies abound on the positive impact that nature has on our bodies and our minds. A short walk in green space reduces blood pressure and stress, while forest bathing (walking in woodland) has been proven to boost our immune system and raise our levels of wellbeing.

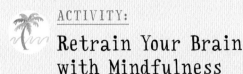

ACTIVITY:

Retrain Your Brain with Mindfulness

Sometimes, it is our own response we need to recover from. Our automatic fight-or-flight response can hijack our mind as it puts the emotional part of the brain in control and prevents us from accessing the rational part.

We can recover more quickly from this state of stress and anxiety when we practise mindfulness. Regular practice (ideally for 30 minutes per day for 8 weeks) tunes up our resilience circuitry, helping us recover from distress faster.

Try this mindfulness meditation:

- Find a comfortable place to sit with no distractions (phone off, door shut).

- Focus your attention on your breathing and the sensation of inhaling and exhaling. Do this for the first breath, and the next, and so on. There is no need to change or judge your breathing in any way, just focus your awareness on it.

As thoughts, ideas and sounds appear and distract you from your breath (and they will), accept them, let them float past and bring your attention back to your breath.

Returning to the breath is the core of this practice. It's not about emptying your mind, it's about training your mind to focus on your breathing, so you can slow down and become mindful about the present moment.

Another way to be mindful is to focus in this moment on what you can hear, see, feel, touch and taste. Focusing on your senses like this is a wonderful way to ground you in the present moment – a useful tool to stop your emotional brain from worrying about the future or ruminating on the past.

Journal and Read

Therapeutic writing is another useful recovery tool. It has been shown to help make sense of crises and provide meaning and a pathway for growth.

According to psychologist Joe Kasper, 'translating emotional events into words leads to profound social, psychological and neural changes.'

Put pen to paper. Write down your ruminations. Express your feelings on the page. Tell your story. This helps to avoid the suppression and inhibition that contributes to depression after trauma. By writing in a story-like format, it's easier to make sense of what you've been through and find a sense of resolution.

Get inspired by other people's stories. Read about people who've overcome the odds and battled through adversity. We can draw strength from taking in true tales of courage and resilience, as we feel inspired to go out there and take on whatever hurdles we encounter in our own life.

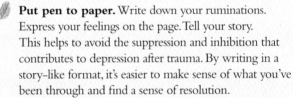

4. How to Rise

'When one door of happiness closes, another opens; but often we look so long at the closed door that we do not see the one which has been opened for us.'

HELEN KELLER

Bounce Forward

Life can deliver brutal blows. Yet, in the wake of tragedy or disappointment, injury or illness, loss or rejection, failure or overwhelm, it is possible, not only to recover and rise, but to grow.

It is possible, not only to bounce back, but to bounce *forward*.

But how?

The first steps are to respond and recover; the next step is to rise.

Or, to put it another way, the first step is to survive; the second step is to grow.

Post-traumatic Growth

It may sound unlikely that people are able to grow following a trauma, yet the potentially transformative impact of suffering has long been known, as written in ancient Hebrew, Buddhist, Christian and Islamic texts and teachings. However, it wasn't until the mid-Nineties that this positive impact was given a name: post-traumatic growth (PTG).

Previously, when studying trauma, psychologists noted two potential outcomes.

1. People experienced debilitating depression and anxiety and/or developed PTSD (post-traumatic stress disorder), which left them struggling to function.

2. People showed resilience and bounced back to where they had been, psychologically, before the trauma occurred.

However, after studying survivors of trauma more closely, a third possible outcome became apparent.

3. People 'bounced forward'. They grew and they thrived following the trauma.

In research studies, while 15 per cent of those who'd suffered trauma developed PTSD, between 60 and 90 per cent of survivors reported at least one positive change since the event, such as having a renewed appreciation for life.

Scientists discovered that with PTG the following five positive psychological shifts occurred as a result of people's struggle with their new reality following a trauma:

1. Greater personal strength.

2. Greater appreciation.

3. Deeper relationships.

4. Renewed sense of meaning in life.

5. Renewed sense of new possibilities.

This personal process of change in how people thought and related to the world in the aftermath of the trauma is what led to the PTG, rather than the trauma itself. Reports of these growth experiences far outweigh reports of PTSD.

Finding Personal Strength

Survival strengthens us. Ever since the philosopher Friedrich Nietzsche concluded 'that which doesn't kill us, makes us stronger,' we've known this to be true. When we survive something difficult, it strengthens our inner resolve and our faith in our own strength.

In their 2010 research paper, '*Whatever Does Not Kill Us: Cumulative Lifetime Adversity, Vulnerability, and Resilience*', M D Seery, E A Holman and R C Silver reveal those who have *some* hardships to handle in their lives tend to have higher levels of wellbeing and life satisfaction than those who've had a comparatively carefree life.

Evidently, good can be found amid the bad.

Indeed, each time we overcome an obstacle, we provide ourselves with evidence of our resilience.

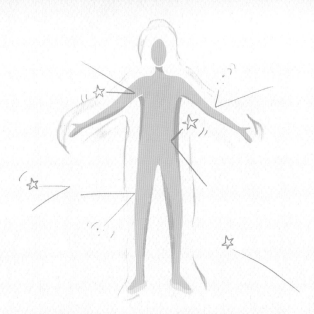

You're Stronger Than You Think You Are

We live through things we never thought we could. And doing so serves as a reminder that we can, we did and we shall again. Survival provides proof of our resilience.

Each time we flex and build our resilience muscles, we prove to ourselves that we can cope. This builds our self-efficacy and amplifies the encouraging feeling that we will be OK.

ACTIVITY:
Proof of Resilience

The hardest thing I've ever had to deal with is ....
....

I'm still here. I survived.

I've experienced (write down some negative emotions
you've felt, such as anger, sadness, grief or guilt)...............
....

I've also experienced (write down some positive emotions
you've felt, such as love, happiness, gratitude and awe).......
....

Some challenges/obstacles/traumas/hardships I've endured
include..
....
....

But here I am.

What I've learned from those adversities is.....................
....
....

And so I'm stronger and better equipped to cope as a result.

Gaining Appreciation

Often, we feel that life will never be the same after we've suffered trauma. The likelihood is, it won't, but this needn't be a bad thing, and often isn't.

Often, we rise with a fresh perspective.

For example, it's reported that survivors often stop 'sweating the small stuff'. We may complain less. Something which generated angst in us before no longer feels like such a big deal. Problems become relative and, as such, less problematic. We put them into perspective and view life through a new lens – one of appreciation.

After enduring adversity, we often appreciate life more and take things for granted less. We notice and feel gratitude for things and experiences and people that we had previously been complacent about. Consequently, we cherish moments and milestones more.

Coming close to dying can teach us some powerful lessons about living. When death enters our awareness, it's a natural response to appreciate being alive. Such lessons about life tend only to be learned from the death of someone close.

Having been shot in the head by the Taliban, human rights activist Malala Yousafzai is incredibly lucky to be alive. Her mother helped remind her daughter of this by giving her birthday cards which celebrated her life after near-death. One year following this traumatic event, Yousafzai received her Happy 1st Birthday card, and so it continues.

Survivors of near-death experiences, people who have very nearly died, who are 'lucky to be alive', have a fresh perspective about living. They get to live. They very nearly didn't. So they value life, and all its ups and downs, far more.

Shifting our perspective from 'I've got to' to 'I get to' is a wonderful way to switch from seeing the inconvenience in a situation to finding the good. This boosts our positive emotions and gives us a renewed sense of appreciation.

For example, say you've got a mountain of laundry or paperwork to get through but it's time to collect your children from school. You might complain, 'I've got to collect the kids now!' But, if you replace that with, 'I *get to* collect the kids from school,' you more readily see why it's a blessing. 'I get to collect the kids from school. Many parents don't get the opportunity to spend this time with their children because of long working hours, but I get to!'

Try it.

ACTIVITY:
Finding the Good

List tasks that often feel like an inconvenience, especially when you're busy.

I've GOT to ....
....
....
....
....
....

Now find the good in those situations. Look at them through a fresh lens of appreciation:

I GET to ....
....
....
....
....
....

Developing an Attitude of Gratitude

When we focus on what we have, rather than on what we haven't; when we notice what's right, rather than what's wrong, we build our level of gratitude and appreciation. This, in turn, pours more positive emotion into our reserves of positivity, which, as Barbara Fredrickson discovered via her broaden and build theory (see page 22), we can draw from when we are experiencing the stresses of life. As such, gratitude helps us to **recover** more quickly from setbacks.

Indeed, practising gratitude has been shown to be the most effective way to reprogramme our negatively biased wiring. Gratitude has been called nature's antidepressant. According to neuroscientist Rick Hanson in his book *Hardwiring Happiness*, when people intentionally practise gratitude, the flow of favourable neurochemicals in the brain multiplies and the neural structure of the brain is literally re-sculpted.

Whether we focus on regret and resentment or on gratitude and appreciation, new neural substrates build up and new synapses grow. And we don't need to wait until we've experienced a trauma in our lives either. We can develop an attitude of gratitude in our daily lives, starting TODAY.

The key lies not just in seeking and finding the good, but in sustained attention on what is good. In order to have the greatest impact, gratitude is a five-step process:

1. **Seek out the good**. Look for it. Pay attention to what's around you. Try using gratitude as a photo prompt and photograph everything you feel grateful for. Seek it out – because searching for the good has been proven to be as effective as finding and appreciating it.

2. **Express gratitude**. Record what you've found to be grateful for in a gratitude photo album, gratitude jar (where you jot down what you're appreciating on a piece of paper and pop it into a jar for reading at the end of the month or year) or gratitude journal.

   If using the latter, write down three good things that went well today as often as you can without it becoming a chore. Next, consider why those things happened. This will help you to focus on the actual sources of goodness, and on how each good thing made you feel.

Write thank-you letters to people and go one step further by delivering them in person and reading them out. This is known as a 'gratitude visit' and is, according to co-founder of positive psychology, Martin Seligman, one of the most effective happiness-boosting exercises anyone can do.

3. **Savour that feeling of gratitude for at least ten seconds.** Notice where in your body you feel that emotion. How does it feel? Savouring in this way installs the positive experience into your memory bank and, by taking your appreciation from your mind to your body and back to your mind again, optimizes the experience. Indeed, neuroscientists have discovered that the longer we spend savouring good experiences and positive feelings, the more our neurons fire and wire together, to reshape our brains for the better.

4. **Go on a gratitude walk.** With each step notice anything around you that you appreciate and then stop, breathe and think about everything in your life right now that you are grateful for. As you breathe slowly in and out, and with each step you take, say thank you to all that brings you feelings of gratitude.

5. **Reminisce about those good moments and memories**. By first anticipating a happy event, then savouring and enjoying it as it happens, and finally recalling that happy memory by reminiscing, we can amplify a solitary magical moment and get the most from the experiences we are grateful for.

Of course, intense sadness still exists and comes in waves, but we can stop ourselves from drowning. Gratitude for what we have, and meaning for what we still have to live for, become life rafts. And, as we devote time to thanking people in person, via letter or simply thinking about or recording what we're appreciative of, the waves still and sadness becomes background noise rather than high-volume surround sound.

Deepening Relationships

Human beings need supportive relationships. They are an essential source of our happiness and mitigate stress.

A 75-year-long Harvard study of 724 adult men concluded that 'good relationships keep us happier and healthier'. Specifically, brains stay healthier, nervous systems relax and emotional pain is reduced when we have someone we can rely on in our lives.

When adversity strikes, emotional support from the relationships we have becomes all the more vital. According to psychologists Krzysztof Kaniasty and Fran Norris, it's not

the actual amount of support provided by those relationships that matters most, but the perception of ongoing support. They discovered we need to feel we have at least one person to count on in times of need. If we do have one person to rely on, we are more likely to be resilient.

Those who experience post-traumatic growth often find that their relationships with key people in their lives deepen and become even more supportive and valued as they embark on their new post-trauma reality.

ACTIVITY:

Who Can You Count On?
(Including Yourself)

In her work with the International Resilience Project, Edith Grotberg created the following four 'muscles of resilience'.

🌿 **I have** (supportive people whom I can trust).

🌿 **I am** (confident, hopeful and aware of my strengths).

🌿 **I can** (solve problems, control myself, learn, bounce back).

🌿 **I like** (participating in activities that lift me up).

These muscles are flexed during post-traumatic growth, and the more we build them, the more resilient we become. So, to flex those muscles, answer the questions opposite and follow the tips below.

🌿 Consider (or ask people directly) what others like best about you and what they think you're especially good at. What situations enable those best qualities to shine?

🌿 Consider ways you can use all the strengths you've listed opposite more often in your daily life.

🌿 Affirm your strengths to bolster your self-belief.

1. **I have...** List your 'inner hut', that is to say, the friends, family and people in your life you feel you can count on to support you...

   ....

   ....

2. **I am...** List your character strengths (for example, hopeful, confident) and skills (what you are good at, such as drawing, listening, organizing).........................

   ....

   ....

3. **I can...** List achievements you are proud of. Consider which strengths and abilities enabled you to achieve those accomplishments, no matter how big or small. Did they require you to be brave, persistent, resourceful or creative? Did you need to be a good listener, organizer, teacher, learner? If so, add these to your strengths list.....

   ....

   ....

4. **I like...** List the activities you enjoy doing, including those that challenge you and make you feel good. Commit to doing them more often.................................

   ....

   ....

Discovering More Meaning

Having lost my mother when I was 17, it wasn't until I was losing my dad as well, over 20 years later, that I realized that by doing work they would both be proud of, I was enabling their story to continue. Losing my mum as a teenager had fostered in me a deep appreciation of life and a fascination with making the most of it. I wanted to help other people to cherish and cope with what they had; to fret less and flourish more. I began researching the field of positive psychology and wrote my first self-help book, on the subject of flourishing in life.

Ironically and tragically, as I was editing the manuscript, out of the blue, I was given the news that my father had been diagnosed with mesothelioma and had mere months to live. He passed away three weeks after his diagnosis. My research on positive psychology and resilience helped me bounce back and forward. And the book and my purposeful mission to enable flourishing became all the more meaningful to me as a result. That, and raising my daughter, became my 'why'.

Purposeful Pain

As Friedrich Nietzsche said, '[S]He who has a why to live for can bear almost any how.'

By choosing to 'forge meaning' and 'build identity' on what they have endured, people can, according to Professor of Clinical Psychology, Andrew Solomon, turn pointless pain into purposeful pain. Says Soloman, you can 'fold the worst events of your life into a narrative of triumph, evoking a better self in response to what hurt.'

In this way it's possible to avoid the chasm of grief by shaping trauma into a catalyst for growth and meaning. Something good can come from something bad. In fact, it often does. Living my life without parents is different from how it would have been had they lived, but I wonder, would I have pursued the same path?

The aforementioned studies on post-traumatic growth (PTG) denote that those who create meaning from their adversities are more likely to be resilient.

Take Joe Kasper, for instance. His son Ryan died in 2011, aged 19, after battling Lafora disease. As Kasper says in his Masters project paper on parental bereavement, 'One of the hallmarks of post-traumatic growth (PTG) is action.' The action Joe took was to study a Masters in Positive Psychology at the University of Pennsylvania. That led him to create a concept in 2013 that he would never have established had it not been for his son's death, a concept he realized could be part of his son's legacy, while helping others to grow after trauma and give his own life more meaning in response to it.

Co-destiny

The therapeutic process that Kasper came up with is called 'co-destiny' – a method to enable growth following the loss of a loved one. It essentially helps survivors continue the story of someone they've lost, in tandem with their own.

Says Kasper, 'Co-destiny is the idea that if you do good in a person's name it adds to that person's legacy. It is a simple yet powerful idea that not only helped me cope with my son's death but enabled me to grow from the tragedy.'

By reframing his response to the trauma and growing through action, Kasper has created meaning in his life that he wouldn't have done, had he not had to endure it. He has given hope to many people who are going through the worst tragedies of their lives.

'The awareness that I could add goodness to my son's life by doing good in his name motivates me to this day,' says Kasper.

Many survivors are able to grow by giving their suffering a purpose. Purposeful pain is easier to bear than pointless pain, experienced in vain.

Meaning in life essentially means that we feel our existence is significant. Significance is more important to our wellbeing than success because it means we matter, whether that's as a teacher, mother, father, writer or any other purposeful role. This enables us to grow and to feel significant. The more we feel we have a positive impact on others, the better we feel as a result.

Or, as neurologist Victor Frankl says, 'In some way, suffering ceases to be suffering at the moment it finds a meaning.'

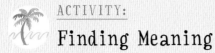

ACTIVITY:
Finding Meaning

Can you attribute some level of meaning from adversity you've faced?...
....
....
....
....
....
....

Meanwhile, what is your own 'why'? For example, your child(ren), your own self-development, helping others in some way?...
....
....
....
....
....
....
....

Seeing New Possibilities

Finding deeper meaning and greater appreciation for life after adversity has a knock-on effect – it helps survivors become more open to possibilities. We want to use our precious time well by contributing to something meaningful.

The possibilities of this new life can motivate and spur us onward. Plan A is replaced with Plans B or C and beyond. Rather than dwelling on what might have been, we can focus on what could be. Rather than expending energy wishing for what was, we can cultivate a new sense of curiosity for what is and who we might become.

Those who grow after a trauma open the door and walk through it into a new life with all of its wonderful possibilities before them.

I hope, in reading this book, you are able to become more open to those possibilities, to rise to the challenges in your life with greater confidence and feel in control of how you respond to them, recover from them and rise above them. As you shift how you think, feel and act in ways that better serve you, may you build your capability to cherish and cope with life, whatever journey it takes you on.

'We don't develop courage by being
happy every day. We develop it by
surviving difficult times and
challenging adversity.'

BARBARA DE ANGELIS

Acknowledgements

Thank you James for being there for me for two decades – your support means more than you know – and Brooke Denise, for being my sunshine when the sky went grey.

Thank you to my soul sisters: Jennie, Peta, Iva, Debra, Tanis, Joanna and Rebecca for seeing, hearing and encouraging me and to 'The Girlies' for your continued support and being there when I needed you most, along with the Hursley Mummas, Ann, Lisa and Ella. Thank you Karen, Helen and Aunty Issy for almost 40 years of friendship. Thank you ALL for the inspiration, compassion, love and laughter. And, most of all, thank you for supporting me to thrive.

Thank you Leanne and Stephanie for believing in me, and Alex and Abi for the epic editing and beautiful illustrations. And thank you Emiliya for your wisdom and positive psychology teaching.

Finally, a posthumous thank you to my amazing mum and dad, Denise and Roger Rickman, for equipping me with all I needed to cope, hope and bounce rather than stay broken. Thank you for giving me a strong back and soft front so that I can help others to fret less, flourish more and, in doing so, create our co-destiny, so that your/our story never ends.